Our Favorite
Maple Syrup
Recipes

Copyright 2024, Gooseberry Patch

Pure maple syrup is labeled with various names according to
strength. Golden is very delicate, perfect for candy making.
Amber has a rich taste you'll love on pancakes and waffles. Dark
and very dark indicates a robust flavor that's just right in baking
and in glazes. They're all delicious!

Maple-Pumpkin Walnut Oatmeal Bake

Serves 10

1 c. canned pumpkin
1 c. milk
2 eggs, beaten
1/2 c. pure maple syrup
1/2 c. brown sugar, packed
1 t. vanilla extract
1 T. cinnamon

1 t. ground cardamom
2 t. baking soda
1/2 t. salt
3 c. old-fashioned oats,
    uncooked
1/2 c. chopped walnuts
Optional: additional 1 c. milk

In a large bowl, mix together pumpkin, milk, eggs, maple syrup, brown sugar, vanilla, spices, baking soda and salt. Stir in oats and walnuts until combined. Spoon into a greased 3-quart casserole dish. Bake, uncovered, at 350 degrees for about 30 minutes, until set. For a make-ahead option, cover and refrigerate overnight. In the morning, uncover, pour one cup additional milk over the top, if desired; bake as directed.

Tuck a packet of Maple-Pecan Muffins into a pretty gift basket
of breakfast foods like flavored coffees, jams & jellies...
a thoughtful gift that's sure to be appreciated.

Maple-Pecan Muffins

Makes one dozen

2 c. all-purpose flour
1/4 c. light brown sugar, packed
1-1/2 t. baking powder
1/4 t. salt
1 egg
1/2 c. milk

1/2 c. maple syrup
1/3 c. margarine, melted
1 t. vanilla extract
1 c. chopped pecans
1 T. sugar
1/8 t. cinnamon

In a large bowl, mix flour, brown sugar, baking powder and salt. In a small bowl, beat egg, milk, syrup, margarine and vanilla. Add egg mixture to flour mixture; stir just until moistened. Batter will be lumpy. Stir in pecans. Spoon batter into paper-lined or greased muffin cups, filling 2/3 full. Mix sugar and cinnamon in a cup; sprinkle over batter. Bake at 400 degrees for 15 to 20 minutes, until golden and a toothpick tests clean. Serve warm.

Post a notepad on the fridge to make a note whenever a pantry staple is used up. You'll never run out of that one item you need!

Maple Whiskey Ribs

1/2 c. pure maple syrup
1/4 c. whiskey or fruit juice
2 T. Dijon mustard

2 lbs. pork spareribs, cut into
  serving-size sections
1 large purple onion, sliced

In a small bowl, whisk together syrup, whiskey or juice and mustard.
Brush mixture over spareribs. Place ribs in a slow cooker; top with
onion slices. Cover and cook on low setting for 6 to 8 hours, until ribs
are very tender.

Candied cranberries are a lovely garnish for roast turkey or
chicken. In a saucepan, bring one cup water and one cup sugar
almost to a boil, stirring until sugar dissolves. Pour into a bowl and
add one cup fresh cranberries; chill overnight. Drain cranberries
well. Toss with superfine sugar to coat and dry on wax paper.

Vermont Maple Chicken

Makes 4 servings

1/4 c. all-purpose flour
salt and pepper to taste
4 boneless, skinless chicken
    breasts
2 T. butter
1/2 c. maple syrup

1 t. dried sage
1/2 t. dried thyme
1/4 t. dried marjoram
1 Spanish onion, sliced
1/2 c. water

Place flour, salt and pepper in a plastic zipping bag. Add chicken to bag and shake to coat evenly; set aside. Melt butter over medium-high heat in an oven-safe skillet. Cook chicken until lightly browned. Remove skillet from heat. Drizzle syrup over chicken, turning to coat completely. Sprinkle chicken with herbs; place onion slices on top to cover chicken. Add water to skillet. Bake, uncovered, at 350 degrees for 30 minutes. Turn chicken over; continue baking for an additional 15 to 20 minutes.

Make breakfast waffle sandwiches for a delicious change.
Tuck scrambled eggs, a browned sausage patty and
a slice of cheese between waffles...yum!

Brown Sugar Cinnamon Waffles

Makes about one dozen

1-3/4 c. buttermilk
1/2 c. butter, melted and cooled
2 eggs, beaten
1-3/4 to 2 c. all-purpose flour
2 T. light brown sugar, packed

2 t. baking powder
1 t. baking soda
1 t. salt
1-1/2 t. cinnamon
Garnish: butter, maple syrup

In a large bowl, whisk together buttermilk, melted butter and eggs; set aside. In another large bowl, whisk together 1-3/4 cups flour and remaining ingredients. Add to buttermilk mixture and whisk until just smooth; add remaining flour if too thin. Let batter stand about 5 minutes. Preheat a waffle iron over medium-high heat; spray with non-stick vegetable spray. Add 1/3 cup batter per waffle to waffle iron; bake according to manufacturer's directions. Garnish as desired.

Save a step by boiling eggs and potatoes at the same time!
Let the potatoes cook in a large pot of boiling water for about
10 minutes, then add the eggs and cook for another 15 minutes.
Remove from heat; drain.

Maple Mashed Sweet Potatoes

Makes 6 servings

5 sweet potatoes, peeled
   and cubed
4 T. extra-virgin olive oil
1 t. salt
1 t. pepper

1/2 c. pure maple syrup
1/4 c. butter, divided
1 sweet onion, sliced
1 T. brown sugar, packed

In a large bowl, toss sweet potatoes with olive oil, salt and pepper. Transfer potatoes to a lightly greased sheet pan; drizzle with maple syrup. Bake at 325 degrees for 30 minutes, or until potatoes are very soft. Meanwhile, melt 2 tablespoons butter in a skillet over medium heat; add onion. Cook for 10 minutes, or until dark golden and caramelized. Remove onion from heat and set aside. Transfer hot potatoes to a serving bowl; mash well. Stir in brown sugar and remaining butter. Heap the caramelized onion on top.

For an easy party spread guests will love, serve up a festive charcuterie board. That's fancy talk for a meat & cheese tray! Arrange a selection of smoked or cured deli meats, cheeses, crackers, nuts, fresh or dried fruits...even some gourmet mustard and preserves for dipping. Delicious and such fun!

Spicy Squash Pickles

Serves 10 to 12

3/4 lb. yellow squash, sliced
   1/4-inch thick
3/4 lb. zucchini, sliced 1/4-inch
   thick
2 t. kosher salt, divided

1/2 c. sweet onion, thinly sliced
1 c. water
1 c. cider vinegar
1/4 c. pure maple syrup
1/4 to 1/2 t. red pepper flakes

Set a wire rack on a baking sheet. Arrange squash and zucchini slices on rack; sprinkle with one teaspoon salt. Let stand 30 minutes; transfer to a colander and rinse well with cold water. Pat dry with paper towels. Combine zucchini, squash and onion in a glass bowl and set aside. In a small saucepan, combine water, remaining salt, vinegar, maple syrup and pepper flakes. Bring to a boil over medium-high heat; stir well and pour over vegetables. Set a plate over vegetables to weigh them down. Refrigerate at least 2 hours or overnight. Drain, or serve with a slotted spoon.

Enjoy seasonal fruits and veggies...strawberries and asparagus in spring, corn and tomatoes in summer, pears and acorn squash in fall and cabbage and apples in winter. You'll be serving your family the tastiest, healthiest produce year 'round.

Maple-Baked Acorn Squash   *Makes 2 servings*

1 acorn squash, halved and   2 t. butter, diced and divided
    seeded   salt and pepper to taste
1/2 c. maple syrup, divided

Fill an ungreased 9"x9" baking pan with 1/2 inch of water. Place
squash halves in pan, cut-side up. Pour 1/4 cup of syrup into each
squash half. Dot each with one teaspoon of butter; sprinkle with salt
and pepper. Cover pan with aluminum foil. Bake at 350 degrees for
about 45 to 50 minutes, until squash is tender.

Save the plastic liners when you toss out empty cereal boxes. They're perfect for storing homemade granola and snack mixes.

Honey Walnut Granola

Serves 12 to 16

3 c. rolled oats, uncooked
3/4 c. chopped walnuts
6 to 8 T. pure maple syrup or
    pancake syrup

6 to 7 T. honey
1/4 c. water
1/4 c. olive oil
3/4 T. vanilla extract

In a large bowl, combine all ingredients together and mix well. Spread out on a greased baking sheet. Bake at 325 degrees for 20 minutes. Remove from oven and stir gently. Bake for another 8 to 10 minutes, or a little longer if a crunchier texture is preferred. Remove from oven and let granola cool completely on baking sheet. Break up and store in a plastic zipping bag or an airtight container.

Cabin-shaped maple syrup tins make whimsical candleholders for the breakfast table. Tuck tapers into the openings and arrange in a group.

Apple Pie Breakfast Bake

Makes 8 servings

2 11-oz. tubes refrigerated
    French bread dough
1 c. butter, melted
21-oz. can apple pie filling
14-oz. can sweetened
    condensed milk

1 t. apple pie spice
1 t. vanilla extract
1 c. pure maple syrup, warmed

Place both loaves of dough seam-side down on a greased baking sheet, side by side. Cut 4 diagonal slashes in each loaf with a sharp knife. Bake at 350 degrees for 26 to 30 minutes, until deeply golden. Cool for 20 minutes. Cut loaves into 1/2-inch cubes to measure 7-1/2 cups; set aside. (Half of one loaf may be left; reserve for another use.) Spread melted butter in a lightly greased 13"x9" glass baking pan; evenly layer pie filling and bread cubes in pan. In a bowl, stir together condensed milk, spice and vanilla until well blended. Spoon over bread, gently pressing bread down to absorb milk. Bake, uncovered, at 375 degrees for 25 to 35 minutes, until bubbly and deeply golden. Let stand for 15 minutes. Serve warm with maple syrup.

The crackle of a warm, cozy fire brings everyone together.
Enjoy a simple dinner of roasted hot dogs or toasty pie-iron
sandwiches and mugs of warm spiced cider in front of the
fireplace. A pan of Baked Stuffed Apples in the oven for dessert
will fill the house with a delicious scent.

Baked Stuffed Apples

Makes 4 servings

4 Granny Smith apples
1/3 c. chopped walnuts
1/3 c. sweetened dried cherries
   or cranberries
1/3 c. brown sugar, packed

1-1/2 t. pumpkin pie spice
1/4 c. pure maple syrup
1 T. butter, melted
1/2 c. apple juice
Optional: vanilla ice cream

With an apple corer, scoop out the core and seeds of each apple from the top. Make the opening fairly wide and do not cut through to the bottom. Set aside. In a bowl, mix together walnuts, cherries or cranberries, brown sugar and spice. Stuff apples full of the mixture; arrange in a 9"x9" glass baking pan. Combine maple syrup and butter in a cup; drizzle over apples. Pour apple juice around apples. Cover with aluminum foil; bake at 350 degrees for 40 minutes. Uncover; bake for about 20 minutes longer, until bubbly and very tender. Serve warm, garnished with a scoop of ice cream, if desired.

Fresh sweet potatoes can easily be used in place of canned.
Just cut them into bite-size pieces and microwave
for five minutes or until tender. Peel each piece and
add to recipe as usual.

Maple-Cranberry Turkey

Makes 4 servings

1-lb. pkg. turkey breast
    tenderloins
1/3 c. sweetened, dried
    cranberries
1/4 c. orange juice

1/3 c. maple syrup
1 T. butter
1/4 t. cinnamon
23-oz. can sweet potatoes,
    drained

Brown turkey in a skillet over medium heat; set aside. In a saucepan, heat cranberries, orange juice, syrup, butter and cinnamon until boiling; remove from heat. Add sweet potatoes to the turkey tenderloins in the skillet; pour cranberry mixture over top. Cover and cook over low heat for 10 minutes; uncover and cook until sauce thickens, about 5 more minutes.

The prettiest linens can often be found at bargain prices during a busy auction. Even if they're slightly worn, beautiful handmade napkins and pillowcases can easily be turned into one-of-a-kind pillow covers, table runners or cafe curtains!

Maple Nut Bread

Makes 8 servings

2 c. all-purpose flour
4 t. baking powder
1 t. salt
3/4 c. milk

1/4 to 1/2 c. maple syrup
1 egg, beaten
1 c. chopped nuts or raisins

Stir flour, baking powder and salt together. Blend in milk, syrup and egg. Add nuts or raisins, mixing well. Pour into a greased 9"x5" loaf pan; bake at 350 degrees for one hour.

Dip to go! Spoon some creamy vegetable dip into a tall plastic cup and add crunchy celery and carrot sticks, red pepper strips, cucumber slices and snow pea pods. Add a lid and the snack is ready to tote. Be sure to keep it chilled.

Laura's Awesome Onion & Cucumber Dip

Serves 12 to 16

1-1/2 c. sour cream or plain Greek yogurt
8-oz. pkg. cream cheese, softened
1/2 c. mayonnaise
3 T. pure maple syrup

1.35-oz. pkg. onion soup mix
1 large English cucumber, peeled and diced
sliced vegetables, crackers, pretzels or chips

In a large bowl, combine sour cream or yogurt, cream cheese, mayonnaise, maple syrup and soup mix. Beat with an electric mixer on medium speed until smooth; stir in cucumber. Cover and refrigerate at least 4 hours. Serve with a variety of fresh vegetables, crackers, pretzels or chips.

Show kids how Grandma & Grandpa used to pop corn, in an old-fashioned hand-cranked popper on the stovetop. They'll love it.

Pumpkin Spice Popcorn

Makes 5 cups

2 T. brown sugar, packed
2 T. pure maple syrup
1-1/2 t. pumpkin pie spice

1 T. butter
5 c. popped popcorn
Optional: 1/2 c. chopped pecans

In a large saucepan, combine brown sugar, maple syrup and spice over medium heat. Cook and stir for 3 minutes, or until bubbly and brown sugar is dissolved. Stir in butter until melted. Add popcorn and pecans, if using; stir until well coated. Allow mixture to cool before serving. Store in an airtight container.

Whip up a luscious topping to dollop on French toast and waffles...
yum! Combine 3/4 cup whipping cream, 2 tablespoons softened
cream cheese and one tablespoon powdered sugar. Beat with
an electric mixer on medium speed until soft peaks form.
Keep refrigerated in a small covered crock.

Stuffed French Toast

Serves 10 to 12

8 thick slices Italian bread,
    cubed and divided
2 8-oz. pkgs. reduced-fat cream
    cheese, cubed
1 to 2 21-oz. cans light cherry,
    blueberry or peach pie filling

1 doz. eggs, beaten, or
    equivalent egg substitute
2 c. skim milk
1/3 c. pure maple syrup
1/8 t. nutmeg or cinnamon

Spread half of the bread cubes in a greased 13"x9" baking pan. Scatter cream cheese cubes over bread. If using 2 cans pie filling, partially drain. Spoon pie filling evenly over cream cheese. Top with remaining bread. In a bowl, whisk together remaining ingredients; pour over bread and cheese. Cover and refrigerate overnight. Bake at 375 degrees for 45 minutes, or until hot and eggs are set.

For an easy fall centerpiece, hollow out shiny red apples and tuck tea lights inside. Arrange on a cake stand and surround with greenery...sweet and simple!

Maple Pecan Pie

Makes 8 servings

14-oz. can sweetened
   condensed milk
3/4 c. maple syrup
2 eggs, beaten

1 c. toasted chopped pecans
9-inch graham cracker crust
Garnish: frozen whipped
   topping, thawed

In a large heavy saucepan, combine condensed milk, syrup and eggs. Bring to a boil over high heat. Reduce heat to medium-low and boil for 5 minutes, stirring constantly. (Be careful, as mixture scorches easily.) Add pecans and mix well. Pour mixture into graham cracker crust. Set aside to cool completely. Cut into wedges and top with whipped topping.

A baker's secret! Grease muffin cups on the bottoms and just
halfway up the sides. Muffins will bake up nicely puffed on top.

Maple-Cream Cheese Muffins

Makes 10 muffins

1/4 c. cream cheese, softened
2 T. pure maple syrup
1-1/2 c. all-purpose flour
1/2 c. whole-wheat flour
2 t. baking powder
1/2 t. baking soda

1/2 t. salt
1-1/4 c. buttermilk
1/4 c. canola oil
2 egg whites, beaten
1/4 c. sugar

In a small bowl, beat together cream cheese and syrup; set aside. In a large bowl, sift together flours, baking powder, baking soda and salt; set aside. In another bowl, whisk together buttermilk, oil, egg whites and sugar; add to flour mixture and stir all together. Spoon batter into greased muffin cups, filling 1/4 full. Drop a teaspoonful of cream cheese mixture into the center of each muffin; add remaining batter to fill cups 2/3 full. Bake at 375 degrees for 20 to 25 minutes.

Sturdy, vintage mugs are great for serving
hot beverages. They hold the heat well...wonderful
to wrap chilly fingers around!

Debi's Maple Hot Chocolate

Makes 4 servings

1/4 c. sugar
1 T. baking cocoa
1/8 t. salt
1/4 c. hot water
1 T. butter

4 c. milk
1 t. maple flavoring
1 t. vanilla extract
12 marshmallows, divided

Combine sugar, cocoa and salt in a large saucepan. Stir in hot water and butter; bring to a boil over medium heat. Add milk, maple flavoring, vanilla and 8 marshmallows. Heat through, stirring occasionally, until marshmallows are melted. Ladle into mugs; top with remaining marshmallows.

Serve warm or chilled cider in old-fashioned Mason jars!
Setting the jars inside wire drink carriers makes it easy
to tote them from kitchen to harvest table.

Praline Mustard-Glazed Ham *Makes 12 servings*

7 to 8-lb. bone-in, smoked
    spiral-cut ham half
1 c. maple syrup
3/4 c. brown sugar, packed
3/4 c. Dijon mustard

1/3 c. apple juice
1/4 c. raisins
1 tart apple, cored, peeled and
    thinly sliced

Remove and discard skin and any excess fat from ham. Place in a
lightly greased 13"x9" baking pan; insert a meat thermometer in thickest
part of ham. Combine syrup, brown sugar, mustard and apple juice; pour
over ham. Set pan on lowest oven rack. Bake at 350 degrees, basting
with drippings every 20 minutes for 2-1/2 hours, or until thermometer
reads 140 degrees. Let ham stand for 10 minutes; remove from pan to a
platter, reserving drippings. Use a bulb baster to remove and discard fat
from drippings. To make sauce, heat drippings with raisins and apples in
a small saucepan over low heat for 5 minutes. Serve sliced ham with
warm sauce.

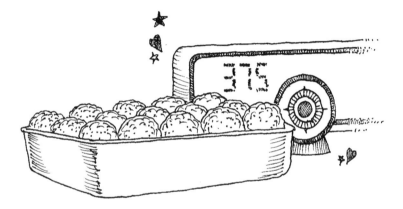

Making a big batch of meatballs? Brown them the easy way...
simply place meatballs in a roasting pan and bake for
15 to 20 minutes at 375 degrees.

Championship Meatballs

1 lb. ground pork sausage
1/2 c. apple butter

1-1/2 T. maple syrup

Form sausage into one-inch balls; place on a microwave-safe plate.
Cover and microwave on high setting for one to 2 minutes, or until a
meat thermometer reads 160 degrees; drain. Cool; place in a plastic
zipping bag. Combine apple butter and syrup; pour over meatballs.
Refrigerate overnight. Shortly before serving, transfer meatballs and
sauce to a microwave-safe serving dish. Cover and microwave on high
for one minute, or until heated through. Serve immediately.

Whenever you shop for cookie cutters, candy sprinkles and other baking supplies, toss a few extras in the shopping cart. Soon you'll be able to fill a gift basket for a friend who loves to bake....she'll really appreciate your thoughtfulness!

Maple Cream Candy

Makes 2 dozen

1 c. pure maple syrup
1 c. sugar

1/2 c. whipping cream
1 T. butter

Combine all ingredients in a heavy saucepan. Cook over medium-low heat until sugar dissolves, stirring occasionally. Cook to soft-ball stage, or 234 to 243 degrees on a candy thermometer. Remove from heat; beat until cool and creamy. Pour into a buttered 8"x8" baking pan. Cool until set; cut into squares.

For a great morning time-saver, keep frozen
chopped onions and peppers on hand.

Maple-Glazed Breakfast Links

Serves 10

2 6-oz. pkgs. precooked
   breakfast sausage links
1 c. pure maple syrup

1/2 c. brown sugar, packed
1 t. cinnamon

Brown sausage links in a skillet according to package directions; drain. Combine remaining ingredients in a bowl; drizzle over sausages. Bring to a boil. Reduce heat to medium-low. Simmer, uncovered, until sausages are glazed.

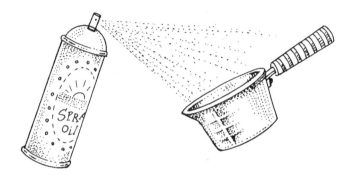

When measuring sticky ingredients like honey or peanut butter, spray the measuring cup with non-stick vegetable spray first. The contents will slip right out and you'll get a more accurate measurement.

Nut & Honey Potato Salad

Serves 4 to 6

1-1/2 c. mayonnaise
1/4 c. brown sugar, packed
2 T. applesauce
2 T. cinnamon
2 T. honey

2 T. maple syrup
1-1/2 lbs. sweet potatoes,
    peeled, boiled and diced
8-oz. pkg. chopped pecans,
    toasted

Combine all ingredients except sweet potatoes and pecans in a large bowl; mix well. Add potatoes and pecans; toss well to mix. Chill for several hours before serving.

Fill a vintage teakettle with mulling spices and cinnamon sticks, then fill with water. Let it gently simmer on the stove so the sweet fragrance will fill your home.

Cinnamon-Maple Nog

6 c. milk
1 c. maple syrup
2 t. cinnamon

2 t. allspice
Optional: 6 4-inch cinnamon
sticks

Combine milk and syrup in a saucepan; warm over medium-low heat,
until heated through. Stir in cinnamon and allspice; serve hot.
Garnish with cinnamon sticks, if desired.

If you like your cornbread crisp, prepare it in a vintage sectioned cast-iron skillet. Each wedge of cornbread will bake up with its own golden crust.

Vermont Maple Cornbread

Makes 9 servings

1-1/3 c. all-purpose flour	1 c. milk
2/3 c. cornmeal	1/3 c. pure maple syrup
1 T. baking powder	1/4 c. butter, melted
1/2 t. salt	2 eggs, lightly beaten

In a large bowl, combine flour, cornmeal, baking powder and salt; mix well. Add remaining ingredients; stir just until combined. Batter will be lumpy; do not overmix. Pour batter into a greased 8"x8" baking pan. Bake at 400 degrees for 25 to 30 minutes, until golden and a toothpick inserted in the center tests clean. Cut into squares; serve warm.

Pick up a couple pints of cinnamon ice cream when it's available...
perfect for adding that special touch to holiday desserts.

54

Maple-Cranberry Pudding Cake

Serves 6 to 8

2 c. fresh or frozen cranberries
1 c. pure maple syrup
2/3 c. whipping cream
3/4 t. orange zest
2/3 c. all-purpose flour
1/3 c. cornmeal
1-1/2 t. baking powder
1/2 t. salt

1 egg, beaten
3 T. sugar
1/2 c. milk
1/2 c. butter, melted
1 t. vanilla extract
Garnish: whipped cream or
    vanilla ice cream

In a saucepan over medium heat, combine cranberries, maple syrup, cream and orange zest. Bring to a boil, stirring occasionally. Reduce heat to medium-low; simmer for one minute and remove from heat. In a bowl, whisk together flour, cornmeal, baking powder and salt; set aside. In a large bowl, whisk together egg and sugar. Add milk, melted butter and vanilla to egg mixture. Add flour mixture to egg mixture; whisk to blend. Pour warm cranberry mixture into a greased 8"x8" baking pan; pour batter over top. Bake at 400 degrees for about 28 minutes, until golden and bubbly at the edges. Cool for 15 minutes. Serve topped with whipped cream or vanilla ice cream.

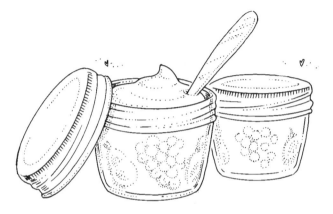

Half-pint Mason jars are just right for filling with layers of fresh fruit, creamy yogurt and crunchy granola. They can even be popped into the fridge the night before, then topped with cereal just before serving. Add a spoon and breakfast is served!

Maple Crunch Oatmeal

Makes 4 servings

1/4 c. chopped almonds
1/3 c. chopped walnuts
2 T. sunflower kernels
1/2 t. cinnamon
1/4 t. nutmeg
1 T. butter, melted

6 T. pure maple syrup, divided
4 servings favorite oatmeal
1/2 c. sweetened dried
    cranberries
Garnish: milk

Combine nuts, sunflower seeds, spices, butter and 2 tablespoons
maple syrup in a bowl; mix well. Spread in a single layer on a
parchment paper-lined baking sheet. Bake at 375 degrees for about
12 minutes, stirring every 5 minutes, until mixture is fragrant and
toasted. Remove from oven; cool. Meanwhile, prepare oatmeal
according to package directions; stir in cranberries and remaining
maple syrup. To serve, divide oatmeal into 4 bowls; divide glazed
nut mixture among bowls and top with milk.

Mix up a zesty Dijon dressing in an almost-empty mustard jar...
delicious on crisp salads, steamed vegetables and broiled fish.
Add 1/2 cup olive oil and 1/3 cup fresh lemon juice to the jar;
shake well. Add salt and pepper to taste. Keep chilled.

Maple-Curry Pork Roast

Makes 6 servings

1-1/2 lb. pork tenderloin
1/2 c. maple syrup
2 T. soy sauce
2 T. catsup
1 T. Dijon mustard

1-1/2 t. curry powder
1-1/2 t. ground coriander
1 t. Worcestershire sauce
2 cloves garlic, minced

Place roast in a large, heavy-duty plastic zipping bag; set aside. Whisk together remaining ingredients in a medium bowl. Pour over roast; refrigerate for at least one hour. Transfer roast with marinade to an ungreased 13"x9" baking pan; bake, uncovered, at 350 degrees for 40 minutes. Let roast stand for 10 minutes; slice thinly and drizzle with sauce from pan.

Fill up a big party tray with colorful crisp veggies for dipping. Calorie-counting friends will thank you!

Surprise Fries

2-lb. butternut squash, halved
    lengthwise, seeded and
    peeled
2 t. olive oil
salt to taste

1/2 t. ground cumin
1/2 t. chili powder
1/2 c. sour cream
2 T. maple syrup

Cut squash halves to resemble French fries; slice about 1/2-inch wide
and 3 inches long. Add oil to a large bowl; add squash, tossing to
coat. Line a baking sheet with aluminum foil; spray with non-stick
vegetable spray. Arrange slices in a single layer on top. Bake
at 425 degrees for 35 minutes, or until tender. Combine salt, cumin
and chili powder; sprinkle desired amount over fries. Blend together
sour cream and syrup as a dipping sauce.

Tuck odds & ends of leftover sliced bread, croissants
and even cinnamon rolls into a freezer container. Before long,
you'll have enough for delicious French toast!

Simple French Toast

Makes 6 servings

3 eggs, beaten
2/3 c. half-and-half or
    whole milk
2 T. sugar or pure maple syrup
1 t. vanilla extract
1/4 t. salt

3 T. butter, divided
6 slices white or egg bread,
    crusts trimmed if desired
Garnish: powdered sugar,
    butter, maple syrup

In a shallow bowl, whisk together eggs, half-and-half or milk, sugar or syrup, vanilla and salt; set aside. Melt 2 tablespoons butter in a skillet over medium heat. Dip 2 slices bread into egg mixture on both sides until saturated. Transfer to skillet and cook until golden on both sides. Repeat with remaining egg mixture, bread and butter. Dust slices with powdered sugar; serve with butter and syrup.

Whisk a cup of heavy cream until soft peaks form,
then gently whisk in a tablespoon of maple syrup...heavenly
served over slices of warm pie!

Maple Syrup Cookies

Makes 4 dozen

1 t. baking soda
1 T. milk
1 egg, beaten
1/2 c. plus 2 T. shortening
1 c. maple syrup

3 c. all-purpose flour
1 T. baking powder
1/2 t. salt
1 t. vanilla extract
10-oz. pkg. chocolate chips

Dissolve baking soda in milk; set aside. Stir together egg, shortening and syrup until mixture is smooth. Add flour, baking powder, salt, vanilla and baking soda mixture; blend well. Stir in chocolate chips. Drop by teaspoonfuls onto greased baking sheets. Bake at 350 degrees for 12 to 14 minutes.

The next time you pop popcorn, sprinkle in a bit of sugar to taste...
super-simple kettle corn!

Maple Popcorn

1 c. maple syrup
3 T. butter

1 T. vanilla extract
2 qts. popped popcorn

Combine syrup and butter in a saucepan over medium heat. Cook and stir until mixture reaches the soft-crack stage, or 270 to 289 degrees on a candy thermometer. Remove from heat; add vanilla. Pour over popped popcorn; mix well. Pour onto wax paper and cool completely.

Making roast chicken & veggies for a crowd? Use a large heavy-duty sheet pan...you'll be able to fit a double or even triple recipe onto the pan. Line the pan with aluminum foil for easy clean-up afterwards. Rotate the pan in the oven halfway through baking time. A simple way to feed a lot of folks well!

Maple-Roasted Chicken & Veggies

Makes 4 servings

1-1/2 lbs. chicken thighs and
   drumsticks
poultry seasoning, salt and
   pepper to taste
2 c. sweet potatoes, peeled and
   cut into 1-inch cubes
2 c. carrots, peeled and cut into
   1-inch pieces

1/2 red onion, cut into
   1-inch squares
3/4 c. maple syrup
2 T. olive oil
2 T. fresh thyme, chopped

Arrange chicken pieces in a lightly greased 13"x9" baking pan;
sprinkle with seasonings. Arrange vegetables around chicken. Drizzle
with maple syrup and olive oil; sprinkle with thyme and toss gently
to coat. Cover and bake at 375 degrees for 30 minutes. Uncover; stir
and bake for about 15 minutes longer, until chicken is golden and
and juices run clear when pierced. Cover again and let stand for
10 minutes before serving.

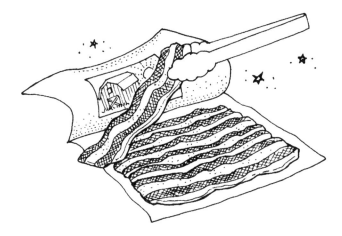

Mmm...is anything better than bacon? To separate
bacon slices easily, first let the package stand at
room temperature for about 20 minutes.

Crispy Maple Bacon

Makes 6 servings

1 lb. sliced bacon   1 t. Dijon mustard
1/2 c. maple syrup

Arrange bacon slices in a single layer. Combine syrup and mustard
in a small bowl; drizzle half of mixture over bacon. Bake, uncovered,
at 400 degrees for 12 to 15 minutes. Turn bacon over; baste with
desired amount of remaining syrup mixture. Bake an additional
5 to 10 minutes, to desired crispness. Drain on paper towels; cool
for several minutes before serving.

A pretty saucer that has lost its teacup makes a useful
spoon rest to set by the stovetop.

Orange-Maple Glazed Yams

Serves 8 to 10

4-3/4 lbs. yams, peeled and
    cut into one-inch cubes
3/4 c. maple syrup

6 T. butter, melted
1-1/2 t. orange zest

Cook yams in boiling water for 3 minutes; drain. Place in a lightly greased 13"x9" baking pan; set aside. Blend syrup, butter and zest; pour over yams. Bake at 350 degrees for 30 minutes, stirring and basting occasionally with syrup mixture. Continue baking for about 15 minutes, until a glaze forms.

Snap up decorative muffin tins...ideal for organizing desk supplies
like push pins, paper clips and rubber bands.

Maple-Glazed Muffins

Makes one dozen

2 eggs, beaten
1-2/3 c. sour cream
1-2/3 c. maple syrup, divided
1 c. all-purpose flour

1 c. bran flake cereal
1 t. baking soda
3/4 c. chopped pecans
6 T. butter, melted

Combine eggs, sour cream and one cup maple syrup; stir in flour, bran flakes, baking soda and nuts. Fill paper-lined muffin cups 3/4 full. Bake at 400 degrees for 15 to 20 minutes. Combine remaining maple syrup and butter; dip muffins in mixture.

A little "magic" for the kids. Put a drop of green food coloring into their milk glasses, then fill with milk as you tap the glasses with a magic wand!

Maple Nut Bars

Makes 16 bars

1-1/2 c. all-purpose flour
2/3 c. sugar
3/4 c. butter
2 eggs, divided
14-oz. can sweetened
    condensed milk

1/4 t. maple flavoring
3/4 c. chopped nuts
3/4 c. semi-sweet chocolate
    chips

Mix flour and sugar together in a large bowl. Cut in butter until it has a crumbly appearance; stir in one egg. Pat into an ungreased 13"x9" baking pan. Bake at 350 degrees for 25 minutes. Combine condensed milk, remaining egg and maple flavoring; stir in nuts. Pour mixture over crust; sprinkle with chocolate chips. Bake for an additional 10 to 15 minutes, until golden and set. Cut into bars.

Use tiered cake stands for bite-size appetizers...so handy,
and they take up less space on the buffet table than
setting out several serving platters.

Maple-Topped Sweet Potato Skins

Makes 12 servings

6 large sweet potatoes
1/2 c. cream cheese, softened
1/4 c. sour cream
2 t. cinnamon, divided
2 t. nutmeg, divided
2 t. ground ginger, divided

2 c. chopped walnuts or pecans
3 T. butter, softened
1/4 c. brown sugar, packed
Garnish: maple syrup, apple
slices, additional nuts

Pierce potatoes with a fork. Bake at 400 degrees or microwave on high setting until tender; cool. Slice each potato in half lengthwise; scoop out baked insides, keeping skins intact. Mash baked potato in a mixing bowl until smooth; add cream cheese, sour cream and one teaspoon each of spices. Mix well and spoon into potato skins. Mix nuts, butter, brown sugar and remaining spices; sprinkle over top. Place potato skins on an ungreased baking sheet; bake at 400 degrees for 15 minutes. Drizzle with warm syrup; garnish as desired.

Ham is so versatile! Serve it as the main dish, or sliced very thin and arranged on split biscuits or bagels, it's an easy-to-eat sandwich. Even leftovers are terrific in soups.

Maple-Brown Sugar Ham

Makes 15 servings

1 c. unsweetened pineapple
   juice
3/4 to 1 c. brown sugar, packed

1/2 c. sugar-free maple syrup
7 to 8-lb. fully cooked ham

Pour pineapple juice into a 7-quart slow cooker. In a small bowl, combine brown sugar and maple syrup. Unwrap ham; discard flavoring packet and if using a bone-in, discard plastic cap. Place ham in slow cooker, flat-side down; pour brown sugar mixture over ham. Cover and cook on low setting for 4 to 5 hours. Baste ham with syrup mixture several times while cooking. Remove ham to a cutting board; let stand 15 minutes before carving.

A flavorful drizzle for steamed veggies...on the stovetop,
simmer 1/2 cup balsamic vinegar, stirring often,
until thickened. So simple and scrumptious.

Maple-Orange Glazed Carrots

Makes 6 servings

3 T. butter, sliced
1/4 c. pure maple syrup
1/4 c. orange juice

1/4 c. water
1/4 t. kosher salt
16-oz. pkg. baby carrots

Melt butter in a saucepan over medium heat. Stir in remaining ingredients except carrots. Add carrots and toss to coat. Bring to a boil over medium-high heat, stirring occasionally. Reduce heat to medium-low. Cover and cook until carrots are tender, about 15 minutes. Serve carrots with sauce from pan.

Handed-down cookie recipes offer a taste of tradition
that just can't be beat. If you weren't lucky enough to receive
recipes from Mom or Grandma, why not check
the cookbook section of your neighborhood library?
It's possible you will rediscover the very recipe
you remember loving as a kid.

Maple Pecan Drops

2 c. all-purpose flour
1/2 c. sugar
1/4 c. brown sugar, packed
1 c. butter, softened

1-1/2 t. maple extract
1/4 t. salt
1 egg, beaten
16-oz. pkg. pecan halves

Combine flour, sugars, butter, extract and salt in a large bowl. With an electric mixer on low speed, beat until blended, occasionally scraping bowl with a spatula. Add egg; blend well. Increase speed to medium; beat until dough is light and fluffy. Roll dough into balls by rounded teaspoonfuls; place about one inch apart on ungreased baking sheets. Gently press a pecan half into the top of each ball. Bake at 350 degrees for 12 to 14 minutes, until lightly golden. Cool cookies slightly on baking sheet; remove to wire racks to cool completely. Store in a tightly covered container for up to 2 weeks.

Stir up a super-simple fruit topping for pancakes and waffles.
Combine a can of fruit pie filling and 2 tablespoons orange juice in
a small bowl. Microwave for 2 to 2-1/2 minutes, stirring twice. Yum!

Nutty Maple Waffles

Makes 8 servings

1-1/2 c. all-purpose flour
2 T. sugar
1 t. baking powder
1/4 t. salt
2 eggs, separated

12-oz. can evaporated milk
3 T. oil
1/2 t. maple extract
1/2 c. pecans, finely chopped

Combine flour, sugar, baking powder and salt in a medium bowl; mix well and set aside. Combine egg yolks, evaporated milk, oil and maple extract in a large bowl; blend well. Gradually add flour mixture, beating well after each addition; set aside. Beat egg whites in a small bowl at high speed with an electric mixer until stiff peaks form; fold into batter. For each waffle, pour 1/2 cup batter onto a preheated, greased waffle iron; sprinkle with one tablespoon nuts. Cook according to manufacturer's instructions.

A no-mess method for greasing and flouring baking pans.
Simply grease pan, sprinkle generously with flour,
cover with plastic wrap and shake!

Chocolate-Maple Muffins

Makes one to 2 dozen

1 c. all-purpose flour
1 t. baking powder
1/2 t. baking soda
1/4 t. salt
2 T. sugar
2/3 c. buttermilk

2-1/2 T. maple syrup
1 egg, beaten
2 T. butter, melted and cooled
  slightly
1 c. mini semi-sweet chocolate
  chips

Grease a 12-cup muffin tin or a 24-cup mini muffin tin. In a large bowl, combine flour, baking powder, baking soda, salt and sugar. In a separate bowl, combine buttermilk, syrup, egg and butter. Add buttermilk mixture to flour mixture; stir well. Fold in chocolate chips. Fill muffin cups 2/3 full. Bake at 350 degrees for 10 to 12 minutes for regular muffins, or 7 to 9 minutes for mini muffins.

Slow cookers come in all sizes, so why not have a couple
on hand? A large-size slow cooker is ideal for family-size
roasts or turkey breasts, while a smaller size is just right
for a savory appetizer dip or fondue.

Slow-Cooker Honey Ribs

Makes 4 servings

10-1/2 oz. can beef broth
3/4 c. water
3 T. soy sauce
2 T. maple syrup
2 T. honey

2 T. barbecue sauce
1/2 t. dry mustard
2 lbs. baby back pork ribs,
    cut into serving-size pieces

Combine all ingredients except ribs in a slow cooker; mix well. Add ribs and stir to coat. Cover and cook on low setting for 6 to 8 hours, or on high setting for 3 to 4 hours.

When buying fresh baking spices, don't discard the old ones...use them in a stovetop potpourri. Add cinnamon sticks and whole cloves to a saucepan of water...toss in apple or orange peels too. Bring to a low simmer, adding more water as needed...delightful!

Ooey-Gooey Baked Apples

Makes 6 servings

6 Gala or Jonagold apples, cored
1/4 c. butter, softened
1/4 c. brown sugar, packed
1/4 c. maple syrup
1 t. cinnamon

1/2 c. raisins
1/2 c. walnuts, finely chopped
Garnish: 16-oz. jar caramel
   ice cream topping

Arrange cored apples in a lightly greased 13"x9" baking pan and set aside. Combine butter, brown sugar, maple syrup and cinnamon in a small bowl; stir in raisins and walnuts. Spoon mixture into center of apples; cover with aluminum foil. Bake at 325 degrees for one hour to one hour and 15 minutes, until apples are tender. Serve warm with caramel topping.

Juicy fresh pears are one of fall's delights. Green Anjou pears and sandy-colored Bosc will hold their shape nicely when cooked, while red or yellow Bartlett pears are delicious for eating out of hand.

Cinnamon Poached Pears

Makes 4 servings

4 pears
1 c. pear nectar
1 c. water
3/4 c. maple syrup

2 4-inch cinnamon sticks,
  slightly crushed
4 strips lemon zest

Peel and core pears from the bottom, leaving stems intact. Cut a thin slice off bottom so pears will stand up; set aside. Combine remaining ingredients in a saucepan. Bring to a boil over medium heat, stirring occasionally. Add pears, standing right-side up. Reduce heat and simmer, covered, for 20 to 30 minutes, until tender. Remove pears from pan. Continue to simmer sauce in pan until reduced to 3/4 cup, about 15 minutes. Serve pears drizzled with sauce.

A centerpiece in a snap! Set a plump pumpkin in the
center of the table and surround with bittersweet vines
and tiny Baby Boo or Jack-be-Little pumpkins.

Maple-Sausage Breakfast Casserole

Serves 6 to 8

1 lb. ground pork sausage
1/4 c. maple syrup
1/4 c. margarine, melted
7 slices country potato bread, torn

8-oz. pkg. shredded Cheddar cheese
5 eggs
1 pt. half-and-half
1 t. salt

Brown sausage in a skillet over medium heat; drain. Reduce heat and stir in syrup; remove from heat. Spread margarine in a 13"x9" baking pan; arrange bread over margarine. Spoon sausage mixture over bread; sprinkle with cheese. Blend together eggs, half-and-half and salt; pour over cheese. Cover and chill for 8 hours to overnight. Uncover and bake at 350 degrees for 40 to 50 minutes.

A basket of homemade scones with a jar of creamy spread makes a tasty gift.

Honey-Maple Biscuits

Makes 2 dozen

2 c. all-purpose flour
1 c. sugar
1 t. baking soda
1/2 t. salt
1 c. sour cream

1 c. butter, softened
1/2 c. honey
1/2 c. pure maple syrup
1 egg, beaten

Combine all ingredients in a large bowl; mix well. Add batter to
24 well-greased muffin cups, filling 2/3 full. Bake at 350 degrees
for 25 minutes, or until tops are golden.

Begin a new and heartfelt Thanksgiving tradition. Ask your
friends & family to bring along an extra food package or can
to dinner, then deliver them to a local food pantry.

Maple-Orange Chicken

Makes 4 servings

2 T. olive oil
4 boneless, skinless chicken
    cutlets, patted dry
salt and pepper to taste
1/4 c. maple syrup

1 T. orange marmalade
juice of 1 lemon
Garnish: chopped fresh parsley
    or sliced green onions

Heat oil in a non-stick skillet over medium-high heat. When hot, add chicken; season with salt and pepper. Cook until chicken is golden on both sides and juices run clear when pierced. Transfer to a warm platter; keep warm. In a small saucepan over medium heat, heat maple syrup until bubbly; stir in marmalade. Simmer until sauce thickens, about one minute. Ladle sauce over chicken; sprinkle with lemon juice. Garnish as desired.

Tag sales and flea markets are the best places to find tea cups, mugs and even kid-size cups. Mixing and matching colors and patterns for serving tea, cocoa or punch is half the fun!

Maple Cream Coffee Creamer   *Makes about 4 cups*

14-oz. can sweetened
   condensed milk
1-1/2 c. milk

1 t. maple extract
1 t. vanilla extract

Combine all ingredients in a blender; mix until well blended. Pour into a
quart-size container; store in refrigerator for up to 2 weeks.

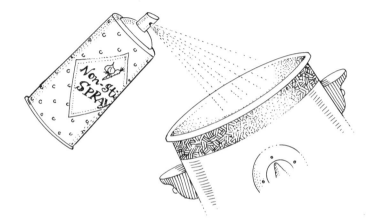

Slow cooking is so easy, keep clean-up a snap too... just spray the inside of the crock with non-stick vegetable spray before adding any ingredients. You can even pick up a handy slow-cooker liner... just toss when it's time to clean up!

Sweet Mesquite Glazed Wings

Makes about 5 dozen

5 lbs. chicken wings
2 T. oil
1/4 c. mesquite seasoning,
    divided

1 c. maple syrup
2 T. lemon juice

Combine wings with oil in a large bowl; toss to coat evenly. Sprinkle with one tablespoon seasoning; toss to coat evenly. Combine syrup, lemon juice and remaining seasoning; set aside. Grill wings over medium-high heat for 15 to 18 minutes, or until juices run clear, turning often. Remove from grill; drizzle with half of syrup mixture. Serve remaining syrup mixture as a dipping sauce.

Go out to greet the sunrise! Wrap warm breakfast breads
in a vintage tea towel before tucking into a basket...
add a thermos of hot coffee or tea.

Mama's Warm Spiced Milk

Makes 4 servings

2-1/2 c. milk
1/3 c. apple butter
2-1/2 T. maple syrup
1/4 t. cinnamon

1/8 t. ground cloves
Garnish: vanilla powder, 4-inch
cinnamon sticks

Whisk ingredients except garnish together in a heavy medium saucepan. Heat over low heat until milk steams (do not boil). Serve sprinkled with vanilla powder and a cinnamon stick for stirring.

Fill a big apothecary jar with penny candy sticks in orange, lemon yellow, golden butterscotch, chocolate brown and other autumn colors. So pretty on a sideboard... invite each guest to choose a favorite!

Maine Maple Candies

Makes 3 dozen

14-oz. can sweetened
    condensed milk
1/4 c. butter, softened
2 T. maple flavoring

1-1/2 c. chopped nuts
32-oz. pkg. powdered sugar
3 8-oz. pkgs. semi-sweet
    chocolate, chopped

Mix together condensed milk, butter, flavoring and nuts; gradually beat in powdered sugar. Roll into one-inch balls. Refrigerate until ready to dip. Melt chocolate in a heavy saucepan over low heat; dip balls into chocolate. Place on wax paper-lined baking sheets until set. Keep refrigerated.

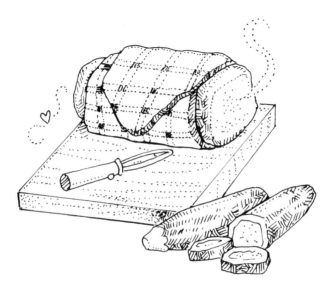

Quick breads taste best when wrapped and stored overnight
at room temperature. They'll slice more easily too!

Wild Rice Bread

Makes 8 servings

2-1/2 c. all-purpose flour, divided
1 pkg. active dry yeast
1/2 t. salt
1 c. water
2 T. butter

2 T. maple syrup
1 egg
1 c. prepared wild rice
1/2 c. chopped pecans

Combine 1-1/2 cups flour, yeast and salt in a large mixing bowl; mix well and set aside. Heat water, butter and syrup in a one-quart saucepan over medium heat until mixture reaches 120 to 130 degrees on a candy thermometer; add to flour mixture. Blend in egg; beat at medium speed until smooth, about 2 to 3 minutes. Stir in remaining flour, rice and pecans by hand; mix well. Spread batter in a greased 2-quart casserole dish; cover and let rise until double in bulk, about 30 minutes. Bake at 375 degrees for 30 to 35 minutes; remove from casserole dish immediately. Cool.

Blend minced garlic, flavored cream cheese or shredded cheese into warm mashed potatoes for a delicious side dish.

Maple-Glazed Turkey Breast

Makes 4 servings

4 potatoes, peeled and cubed
1 onion, chopped
2-lb. boneless turkey breast
1/4 c. maple syrup

1/4 c. apricot preserves
Optional: 1/4 t. cinnamon
1/2 t. salt
1/8 t. pepper

Combine potatoes and onion in a slow cooker; place turkey breast on top. Combine remaining ingredients in a small bowl; mix well. Pour over turkey. Cover and cook on low setting for 6 to 7 hours, until vegetables are tender and turkey registers 180 degrees on a meat thermometer.

If you're baking potatoes for dinner tonight, make them
even tastier by rubbing the skin with softened butter
and salting them before baking!

Maple-Marinated Salmon

Makes 6 servings

3/4 c. maple syrup
2 T. fresh ginger, peeled
   and grated
2 T. lemon juice

2 T. low-sodium soy sauce
1/2 t. pepper
1/4 t. salt
2-1/4 lbs. skin-on salmon fillets

In a greased 13"x9" baking pan, stir together all ingredients except salmon. Place salmon, skin-side up, in pan. Cover and refrigerate 15 minutes. Turn; marinate another 15 minutes. Line a separate 13"x9" baking pan with parchment paper. Place salmon on parchment, skin-side down; brush with marinade. Bake at 400 degrees for 10 minutes. Brush with remaining marinade and return to oven for 10 to 15 minutes, until fish flakes easily with a fork. Discard skin before serving.

Fresh jalapeño peppers are extra flavorful, but take care
when slicing them. It's best to wear plastic gloves,
and be sure not to touch your eyes!

Maple Bacon & Cheddar Jalapeños

Makes about 2-1/2 dozen

8-oz. pkg. cream cheese,
    softened
1 c. shredded Cheddar cheese
1 T. brown sugar, packed

16 jalapeño peppers, halved
    lengthwise and seeded
1 lb. maple bacon, slices cut
    in half

In a bowl, blend cheeses and brown sugar. Spoon one teaspoon of cheese mixture into each pepper half; wrap with bacon and place on a grilling plate. Grill on low grill setting for about 30 minutes, until bacon is crisp and golden. May also place peppers on a baking sheet; bake at 350 degrees for 30 minutes. Makes about 2-1/2 dozen.

Keep a cherished cookbook clean and free of spatters.
Slip it into a gallon-size plastic zipping bag before
cooking up a favorite recipe.

Not Your Granny's Brussels Sprouts

Serves 6 to 8

2 slices bacon, diced
2 lbs. Brussels sprouts, trimmed
    and halved or quartered
1 T. olive oil
1 t. salt

2 T. pure maple syrup
1 t. cider vinegar
1 t. Chinese 5-spice powder,
    or 1/8 t. cinnamon plus
    1/8 t. pepper

In a skillet over medium heat, cook bacon until crisp. Set bacon aside, reserving one teaspoon drippings. In a large bowl, toss Brussels sprouts with reserved drippings, olive oil and salt. Arrange sprouts on a lightly greased baking sheet. Bake, uncovered, at 350 degrees for 15 to 20 minutes, until just tender. Turn oven to broil. Broil sprouts for 2 to 3 minutes, just until slightly charred. Meanwhile, combine syrup, vinegar and spice in a small saucepan; simmer over low heat for several minutes. Toss sprouts with syrup mixture and reserved bacon.

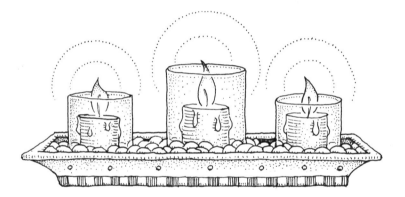

Set lighted votives on a shallow tray filled with glass
pebbles for a quick & easy centerpiece.

Maple-Glazed Chicken & Yams

Makes 4 servings

4-lb. chicken, cut into
  serving-size pieces
1 yellow onion, sliced into
  wedges
2 yams or sweet potatoes, peeled
  and cubed

2 T. olive oil
1 t. salt
1/4 t. pepper
3 T. maple syrup
6 sprigs fresh thyme

Arrange chicken, onion and yams or sweet potatoes in a lightly
greased 13"x9" baking pan. Drizzle with oil; sprinkle with salt and
pepper and toss to coat. Drizzle with syrup; top with thyme. Bake,
uncovered, at 400 degrees for about one hour and 15 minutes, stirring
vegetables once, until chicken juices run clear. Let stand for 10 minutes
before serving.

Invite neighbors over for a fall breakfast...outside around
the fire ring or inside by the fireplace. It's a great way to
catch up with one another.

Country Breakfast Sandwiches

Makes 4 servings

3 T. butter, divided
1 Granny Smith apple, peeled,
   cored and thinly sliced
4 slices whole-wheat bread,
   toasted

3 links pork sausage, halved
   lengthwise and browned
1/4 c. maple syrup, warmed

Heat 2 tablespoons butter in a skillet over low heat. Add apple; sauté until tender and golden, turning often. Spread toasted bread with remaining butter; top each slice with sausages, apple slices and syrup.

Save bananas that are getting too ripe. Peel, cut into chunks, wrap in plastic wrap and tuck in the freezer. Later they can be tossed into smoothies...no thawing needed.

Pumpkin Pie Smoothie

Makes 2 servings

3/4 c. milk or unsweetened
    almond milk
1/2 c. plain Greek yogurt
2 to 3 T. maple syrup or honey
1/2 c. canned pumpkin

1/2 t. vanilla extract
1/2 t. cinnamon
Optional: 1/8 t. nutmeg
1 c. ice cubes

Combine all ingredients in a blender; process until smooth.

INDEX

Our Story

Back in 1984, we were next-door neighbors raising our families in the little town of Delaware, Ohio. Two moms with small children, we were looking for a way to do what we loved and stay home with the kids too. We had always shared a love of home cooking and making memories with family & friends and so, after many a conversation over the backyard fence, **Gooseberry Patch** was born.

We put together our first catalog at our kitchen tables, enlisting the help of our loved ones wherever we could. From that very first mailing, we found an immediate connection with many of our customers and it wasn't long before we began receiving letters, photos and recipes from these new friends. In 1992, we put together our very first cookbook, compiled from hundreds of these recipes and, the rest, as they say, is history.

Hard to believe it's been almost 40 years since those kitchen-table days! From that original little **Gooseberry Patch** family, we've grown to include an amazing group of creative folks who love cooking, decorating and creating as much as we do. Today, we're best known for our homestyle, family-friendly cookbooks, now recognized as national bestsellers.

One thing's for sure, we couldn't have done it without our friends all across the country. Each year, we're honored to turn thousands of your recipes into our collectible cookbooks. Our hope is that each book captures the stories and heart of all of you who have shared with us. Whether you've been with us since the beginning or are just discovering us, welcome to the **Gooseberry Patch** family!

Visit our website anytime
www.gooseberrypatch.com

Jo Ann & Vickie

1·800·854·6673